WORK-RELATED VIOLENCE

Case studies

Managing the risk in smaller businesses

HSE BOOKS

First published 2002

ISBN 0 7176 2358 0

HSE commissioned Poyner Research to gather the
information for the case study material in this book.
We would like to thank them and the companies who
agreed to be involved with the original research.

Contents

Introduction

BACKGROUND

1   Violence at work is a serious problem which affects many people. Physical attacks are the most serious form of violence, but verbal abuse and threats are much more common and can have long-term effects on victims.

2   A recent study, *Violence at work: Findings from the British Crime Survey,* commissioned by HSE, showed that people working in smaller businesses were more likely to be threatened or assaulted at work than people working for large organisations. See the 'Further information' section at the end of this book for details.

3   Working directly with members of the public puts people at higher risk of violence. High-risk occupations include enforcement roles such as bailiffs and security services, or delivering a service to the public - for example, health services, social care and the retail and hospitality trades. Many small and medium-sized businesses are involved in these areas of work.

AIM OF THIS BOOK

4   This book of case studies is mainly for owners and managers of small and medium-sized businesses, but it should also interest employees and safety representatives. A small business is defined as an organisation with less than 50 employees. A medium-sized business has 50-249 employees. The case studies show that the problem of violence at work can be tackled in many ways. They offer real examples of how some businesses have reduced the risk of violence. Although the situations and risks in the case studies may vary, many of the responses and solutions identified will be relevant to businesses in different sectors.

LEGAL REQUIREMENTS

5   Health and safety law applies to risks from violence, just as it does to other risks at work. The main pieces of relevant legislation are:

● **The Health and Safety at Work etc Act 1974**
Requires employers to protect the health and safety of their employees.

● **The Management of Health and Safety at Work Regulations 1999**
Requires employers to:
- consider the risks to employees (including the risk of reasonably foreseeable violence);
- decide how significant these risks are;
- decide what to do to prevent or control the risks;
- develop a clear management plan to achieve this.

● **_The Reporting of Injuries, Diseases and Dangerous Occurrences Regulations 1995 (RIDDOR)_**
Employers must report any incidents involving physical assaults on employees which result in death, major injury or where the employee is unable to carry out normal work for three or more days. RIDDOR does not cover threats and verbal abuse or absence due to emotional trauma.

● **_The Safety Representatives and Safety Committees Regulations 1977 and The Health and Safety (Consultation with Employees) Regulations 1996_**
Require employers to inform and consult safety representatives (where there are recognised trade unions) and employees on health and safety matters.

HSE GUIDANCE

6   HSE has published simple general guidance, _Violence at work: A guide for employers,_ which gives practical advice on how to find out if violence to staff is a problem, and how to tackle it. More detailed guidance is also available for the health services, education, banks and building societies and retail sectors. See the 'Further information' section at the end of this book for more details.

THE CASE STUDIES

7   The case studies have been grouped according to business sectors. The sectors covered by this book are:

● Retail.

● Health and welfare.

● Security and enforcement.

● Leisure/service providers.

8   Each case study describes a particular business, the risks of violence to its staff or owners, measures taken to reduce the risk of violence it faces and additional points about other measures which could have been used, or which may be relevant to other businesses.

Managing work-related violence

EFFECTS OF WORK-RELATED VIOLENCE

9   Work-related violence has serious consequences for employees and for the businesses they work for. Victims may suffer not only from physical injury, but also psychological effects, such as anxiety and stress. For their employers this can represent a real financial cost - through low staff morale and high staff turnover. This in turn can affect the confidence of a business, its profitability and even its viability. Further costs may arise from expensive insurance premiums and compensation payments.

10   Failure to manage the risk of violence can also lead to enforcement action by HSE or the local authority, and even prosecution.

GOOD MANAGEMENT IS GOOD BUSINESS

11   One of the key findings of the work by Poyner Research for the case studies in this book was that many owners and managers of smaller businesses manage the risk of violence very successfully. They have reduced the potential for violence and increased their ability to deal with difficult situations. The business is therefore likely to be more efficient, profitable and able to recruit and retain high quality employees.

12   If a business successfully manages the risk of violence, it will usually manage other risks equally well. In other words, a well-managed business is likely to be a safe business.

13   The case studies show that there is nearly always a range of possible solutions to every problem. In particular, they show that effective measures do not have to be expensive. The most cost-effective solutions usually arise from the way the business is run, such as staff training, reorganising work schedules and the physical environment. High technology, high cost security equipment will normally only be needed where there is a particularly high risk of violence, or to protect premises when they are unoccupied.

MANAGING WORK-RELATED VIOLENCE

FOUR-STAGE MANAGEMENT APPROACH

14   The process of managing the risk of violence is the same as for any other health and safety risk. The key aspects of successful management are to identify the risks and decide what measures can be taken to prevent or control those risks. A straightforward four-stage approach is set out below:

Stage one: Finding out if you have a problem

The best way is to discuss this with your staff, but in small firms most owners will already be aware of problems from personal experience. Think about all the potential risks - look for common causes, areas or times of incidents. Your next steps can then be targeted where they are needed most.

Stage two: Deciding what action to take

There are always a number of possible solutions, so it's important to choose the right one for the situation. You could consider action in three areas:

● Training and information for staff. Can your staff spot the early signs of aggression and either avoid it or calm the situation? Are staff aware of the measures in place to protect them?

● The work environment. Think about the design and layout of your business premises. Could you provide better seating and lighting in waiting areas, or wider counters for reception staff? Where there is a particularly high risk of violence you could consider security equipment such as coded security locks to keep the public out of staff areas, or alarm systems and even video cameras.

● The design of the job. Can working practices and patterns be changed? Examples include:

  -   reduce the risk of robbery by using cheques, credit cards or tokens, and try varying the route to take money to the bank;

  -   check the credentials of clients and the arrangements for meetings away from the workplace;

  -   make arrangements for employees to keep in touch if they are away from their work base;

  -   try to avoid staff working alone.

Stage three: Take action

Make any changes needed and check that employees are following your agreed policy.

Stage four: Check that what you have done is working

You will need to check regularly that your arrangements are working. In smaller businesses these reviews can be informal, but you should make sure that employees are involved in the process. If violence is still a problem, try something else - look for ideas in this book. Circumstances can change so it's important to consider whether other solutions may be more appropriate at a different time.

15   All employers and self-employed people are required by law to make a risk assessment, and this four-stage process covers the main aspects of the legal requirements. Anyone employing five or more people must record the findings of their risk assessment. This record may be put in writing or held some other way (such as on a computer).

16   You may wish to use your risk assessment to help you develop a policy setting out your approach to work-related violence. You could write a formal policy, perhaps combining it with a more general safety policy statement for staff. However, in very small firms it may be more appropriate to explain your ideas verbally to employees.

HELPING EMPLOYEES AFTER AN INCIDENT

17   If there is a violent incident involving your staff you should respond quickly to avoid any serious consequences. It is important to plan how you are going to support employees before any incidents occur. You may want to think about the following options:

● Support - talk to victims about their experiences as soon as they feel ready after the event. Remember that verbal abuse can be just as upsetting as a physical attack.

● Time off work - individuals will react differently and may need different amounts of time to recover. If they continue to feel seriously distressed they may need specialist support.

● Legal help - in serious cases legal help may be appropriate.

● Help for other employees - even those not directly affected by a violent incident may need guidance and/or training to help them deal with feelings of anxiety and to help them cope with similar incidents themselves.

18   The Home Office leaflet *Victims of Crime* gives more useful advice if one of your employees suffers an injury, loss or damage from a crime, including how to apply for compensation. See the 'Further information' section at the end of this book for more details.

19   Victim support schemes operate in many areas. Details of local services can be obtained through the Victim Supportline on 0845 30 30 900 (local call rate number).

Work-related violence case studies: Managing the risk in smaller businesses

SECTOR: RETAIL

Research from The British Retail Consortium estimates that £1.39 billion was lost to retailers in 1998 as a result of crime. The most likely type of violent crime in this sector is robbery. Larger national retailers often have significant resources to improve security and protective measures against violent crime, and it has been suggested that the risk of crime has moved to smaller, more vulnerable outlets.

The British Crime Survey has confirmed that people working in retail sales face higher risks of violence at work - particularly the risk of threatening behaviour from customers. In this sector there is a high level of face-to-face contact with the public and the British Crime Survey identifies several situations in which violence tends to arise. For example, violence may result when staff confront known or suspected shoplifters, either to prevent a theft or in refusing to exchange goods.

Retail case studies

1 Convenience store

2 Pizza delivery

3 Market traders

RETAIL

Case study 1   Convenience store

BACKGROUND

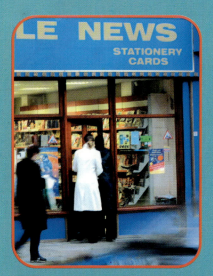

This case study focuses on a family-run convenience store in a small town. The town has a relatively low crime level. The store opens daily from 8 am until 11 pm, has 1000 square feet of sales area and sells newspapers, tobacco, groceries and wines and spirits.

The store is situated on a main road through the town, so it attracts a significant amount of passing trade.

KEY RISKS

- Robbery from staff and theft from the shop.

- Assaults.

- Threats and abuse.

- Dealing with disorder.

Examples of incidents

One incident involved two feuding families. Two men began to fight and the female staff member tried to calm the situation. One man left the shop but later returned with a group of family members to continue the fight. Again the member of staff helped to calm the situation.

A relative of someone believed to be an alcoholic became angry and accused the store of selling drink to the alcoholic. The individual was soon calmed down.

A group of youths tried to steal a bottle of spirits. One of the youths aggressively blocked the way of a staff member who had seen the attempted robbery. The youth appeared to be under the influence of drugs.

Convenience store   Case study 1

REDUCING THE RISK

Training and information

- Staff are trained in basic safety techniques. They are taught:
  - not to put themselves at risk (eg don't resist robberies);
  - to position themselves so they have an escape route; and
  - to summon help and support immediately, if they need it.

- Staff are encouraged to give good service and have a positive attitude.

Work environment

- The amount of high value goods in the shop is kept to a minimum.

- CCTV cameras have led to a successful prosecution for theft.

- A large secure stockroom at the back of the shop holds high value stock.

- Valuable goods are displayed behind or close to the till.

- The till is located next to the shop entrance so that it can be easily seen from the street.

- Staff have a clear view of the entire shop and the street immediately outside.

Job design

- There are always two staff on duty.

OTHER OPTIONS

- Panic alarms on tills, connected to the police station.

- Glass screens across the counter.

- Encourage the local police to make random visits to the shop.

- Reduce the amount of cash held on the premises.

REDUCING THE RISK

RETAIL

Case study 2   Pizza delivery

BACKGROUND

This case study looks at two pizza takeaway and delivery outlets in a suburban parade. The two premises are situated next to another fast food outlet and a restaurant.

The road outside these premises is very busy, and the businesses are open until midnight every day. This generates a high level of activity during trading hours.

KEY RISKS

- Assaults on delivery staff.

- Theft of cash and damage to the delivery vehicle.

- Hoax orders.

- Disorder, threats and abuse in the shops.

- Payment disputes.

Examples of incidents

A delivery bike was stolen late one night on a housing estate, leaving the driver stranded.

At other times vehicles had been moved or hidden on the same estate.

RETAIL

Pizza delivery   Case study 2

RETAIL

REDUCING THE RISK

Training and information

- The businesses have adopted a culture of speedy, cheerful and friendly service to avoid crowding or frustration at being delayed.

- Staff are trained not to react to abuse.

- Staff are told not to resist robbery.

Work environment

- The businesses have large street windows to increase surveillance.

- Delivery bikes are parked against the shop window to keep them in sight.

- The premises and immediate street front are kept clean and well-managed.

- Locks and immobilisers are installed on all delivery vehicles.

- Notices have been placed in the shop and are carried by staff stating that they only hold a small amount of change.

Job design

- The businesses use electronic databases of customers which identify whether an address has been used legitimately before. This helps to avoid repeat hoaxes.

- Phoned orders are monitored for possible hoaxes (particularly those from public call boxes).

- There are always several staff serving at any one time. They remain visible and actively serving.

- Staff may go to problem areas in pairs and/or in an unmarked car (particularly at night).

OTHER OPTIONS

- Ask non–serving staff to work close to the counter to keep an eye on the whole shop.

- Keep public waiting areas small - just large enough for queuing and movement, to stop people loitering inside the shop.

Case study 3   Market traders

BACKGROUND

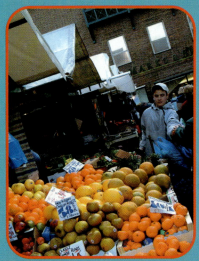

This case study focuses on a street market in a major city. It is a long-established market with traditional street stalls and open-fronted shops at either side. The market opens daily and has 181 pitches, which extend in two rows along the street. The street is long and narrow and the market and shops are usually very busy.

The stalls and open-fronted shops offer a wide range of products including food, clothing, home utensils, toys, electronics and small gifts.

The south side has a direct access to an enclosed market and shopping centre, which is located behind the open-fronted stores. There is also a local police office in the market street to ensure a permanent police presence.

KEY RISKS

- Disorder from groups of people who congregate in the area.

- Intimidation and abuse, including racial harassment.

- Physical assault as a result of moving on pickpockets, drug dealers and unlicensed traders.

- Theft of stock from stalls.

- Theft of cash from stalls or robbery when taking cash to the bank.

Example of incident

A jeweller was threatened with a knife and when he refused to hand over valuable items, he was stabbed. The attacker escaped empty-handed. The shop owner needed hospital treatment, but was able to return to work soon afterwards.

Market traders   Case study 3

REDUCING THE RISK

Training and information

- Stallholders share information about potential troublemakers, particularly if they know that people likely to be violent are in the market area.

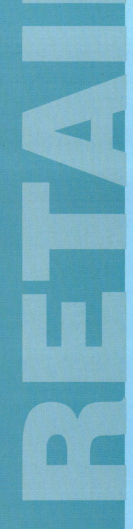

- There is no formal training for stallholders, but the accepted approach is to deal with customers in a friendly way. The 'banter' helps to defuse potential hostility and attracts passers-by to the stall.

- Staff are encouraged to use a range of non-threatening ways of dealing with troublemakers by:
  - not responding to threats of provocation;
  - approaching people with a friendly and relaxed expression;
  - giving people the opportunity to move away without further confrontation (allowing them to 'save face');
  - in a verbal exchange, standing sideways to present a less threatening image and maintaining a relaxed appearance.

Work environment

- Stallholders ensure they avoid blind spots on or around their stalls.

- Valuable merchandise is kept out of reach of customers, or displayed in sealed presentation packs.

- Cash is kept in a secure place.

- Stock not on display is kept secure.

- There are regular patrols by the police and the market inspector.

Job design

- Most stalls have more than one attendant and staffing levels are increased at busy times.

- Stallholders watch over each other and neighbouring stalls, although the crowds of shoppers can make surveillance difficult.

- Staff move to the front of the stall at busy times, or when dealing with valuable goods.

OTHER OPTIONS

- Use of CCTV as a deterrent and to help with prosecutions.

- Better lighting of street and stalls.

- Radio links with the police.

- More police and market inspector patrols.

REDUCING THE RISK

RETAIL

SECTOR: HEALTH AND WELFARE

Health service and social care workers face some of the highest levels of violence of all occupations. Findings from The British Crime Survey show that just over 7% of medical practitioners reported being attacked or threatened at work - almost four times the national average. However, violence is a serious risk for all staff in this sector, and many victims have suffered repeated attacks and abuse.

Violence to health and welfare staff arises primarily because their work involves contact with a wide range of people in circumstances which may be difficult. Attackers may be suffering from physical pain, emotional distress, or mental health problems.

Health and welfare case studies

4 Health centre

5 Drop-in centre

HEALTH AND WELFARE

Case study 4   Health centre

BACKGROUND

The health centre is situated in a suburb of a major city, within a large housing estate. The centre is responsible for 16 500 patients in an area where there are high levels of social deprivation.

The centre is the base for nine general practitioners and other administrative staff, as well as other medical specialists including district nurses, health visitors, chiropodists, dental practitioners and a community psychiatric nurse.

KEY RISKS

- Rudeness, threats, abuse to receptionists - when patients cannot not be seen immediately.

- Rudeness, threats, abuse to medical staff – when the treatment offered does not meet the patients' expectations.

- Physical attacks – when dealing with visitors who are under the influence of alcohol or drugs, or those with mental illness.

Examples of incidents

A young man arrived without making an appointment. The receptionist told him that he would have to wait four hours for the next available appointment. He became very aggressive, banging his fist on the desk and shouting. The practice manager was alerted and defused the situation by moving him out of the reception area. When the young man had calmed down he was scheduled for an earlier appointment which still required him to wait.

Doctors were threatened and abused when a medical certificate requested for time away from work was refused and the treatment recommended did not meet the patient's expectations.

KEY RISKS

HEALTH AND WELFARE

Health centre   Case study 4

REDUCING THE RISK

Training and information

- All staff are made aware of the factors which place them at risk from patients.

- Staff have not been specifically trained to deal with aggression, but the receptionists are experienced in assessing body language and other cues, to identify those who may become violent or abusive.

Work environment

- Individual booths have been installed in the reception area to ensure a level of privacy when dealing with the receptionists.

- Panic alarms are linked to the local police station.

- Telephones are fitted with a button that broadcasts difficult conversations to colleagues.

- External CCTV has been installed, with signs to warn people of its existence.

Job design

- Staff use coded messages to alert other staff to a potential problem.

- A local policeman makes random visits.

OTHER OPTIONS

- Doctors can remove violent and uncooperative patients from their lists. This right can be drawn to the attention of patients, to allow them to modify their behaviour.

- Keep a log of difficult patients to pass to new doctors or locums visiting homes.

- Consider new reception desks to achieve greater privacy (eg with sound proofing) and protection (eg wider desks).

- Make the local community aware of the fact that drugs are not kept on the premises.

- Use a log book to record incidents.

- Provide more formal training in recognising and defusing aggression.

Case study 5   Drop-in centre

BACKGROUND

Drug abuse is often associated with crime and is increasingly a factor in work-related violence. Specialised centres for counselling and care of drug users are likely to be high risk places of work.

This case study gives details of a drop-in centre for drug users in a large city. It is run by a charity which employs a staff of seven and has 12 volunteers. The aim of the centre is to provide drug users, their friends and families with help and advice on drug-related problems. It also provides counselling by professional case workers, funded in part by local authority grants.

The centre is open three afternoons a week from 12 pm to 4 pm (Monday, Wednesday and Friday). Formal casework sessions are done by appointment, using two interview or counselling rooms on the first floor above the entrance.

There is an incident book at the centre, but it is not routinely used. Some incidents are deliberately not recorded, to protect clients' confidentiality.

KEY RISKS

- Assault and verbal abuse from clients.

- Disorder and abuse from members of the public trying to get into the centre.

Examples of incidents

A member of staff was threatened with a bottle when he refused to contact a client's GP for another prescription. This had been done previously, but the centre refused to keep asking on the client's behalf.

People who have been drinking sometimes come to the centre to cause a nuisance. They argue at the door and create a disturbance and some have to be physically removed from the premises.

Drop-in centre   Case study 5

REDUCING THE RISK

Training and information

- Staff adopt a non-confrontational and non-judgemental approach to clients, encouraging clients to talk about their problems.

- Staff are trained to avoid being patronising, to help create an equal balance of power between staff and clients.

- There is a culture of commitment to being helpful to clients.

Work environment

- Light yellow paint has been used to brighten up the premises.

- An informal entry area makes the centre more welcoming. A previously raised reception area was removed to avoid a formal and dominating image.

- The reception desk provides a central control point from which all client-accessible areas can be supervised.

- Counselling rooms are designed to be private, but are within hearing range of reception area.

- Staff offices are located out of sight of clients, and the open-plan layout allows staff to see each other.

Job design

- There is continuous staffing of the reception area when the centre is open.

- Assistance is always available if staff in private counselling rooms need help.

- There are no security technologies aimed at staff protection, only intruder detection systems for use when the building is closed. These are linked to a call centre, the intention being to protect client records kept on computers.

- The centre has close links with the police, but police officers are discouraged from entering the centre unless there is an emergency.

OTHER OPTIONS

- CCTV might be used for extra surveillance, but clients could be concerned about confidentiality.

- Security buttons could be provided for staff to alert colleagues if they feel threatened.

REDUCING THE RISK

HEALTH AND WELFARE

Work-related violence case studies: Managing the risk in smaller businesses

SECTOR: SECURITY AND ENFORCEMENT

Security guards and other protective services have the highest risk of violence of all sectors, with ten times the national average risk of assault and four times the average risk of threats. This sector includes police officers who face extremely high risks of violence, but other similar occupations are also vulnerable.

Security guards and enforcement officers may have a high level of contact with known or suspected criminals, and violence tends to occur while apprehending someone or enforcing the law. Staff may be employed specifically to deal with violent people (eg door supervisors), or to protect other employees or property.

Among some of those in this sector, violence is an expected occurrence and may be regarded as 'part of the job'. For this reason, many incidents may not be reported.

Security and enforcement case studies

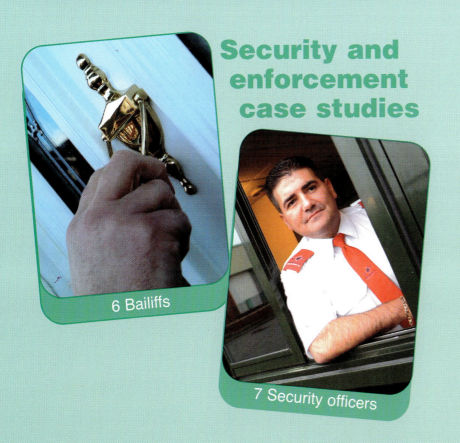

6 Bailiffs

7 Security officers

SECURITY AND ENFORCEMENT

Case study 6   Bailiffs

BACKGROUND

The working environment of bailiffs has a high potential for physical violence and abuse. They generally only come into contact with people after other attempts to resolve a dispute have failed.

This case study focuses on a small commercial practice run by a woman who is an experienced practising bailiff. She has a team of three men and one woman. They have over thirty years combined service as bailiffs and are all certificated with their local County Court.

Assignments for the business include the collection of money, serving notices (injunctions, divorce and bankruptcy petitions, eviction orders etc) and repossession of property.

KEY RISKS

- Assaults, abuse and threats, including those arising from being recognised off duty.

- Damage to cars and property.

- Theft of property and cash.

- Risk of being taken hostage.

- Attacks by dogs.

Examples of incidents

Police were trying to prevent travellers entering onto a common. The officers stopped vehicles while the bailiff served the written notice on the drivers. The encounters were accompanied by swearing, abuse and spitting, and a bucket of urine was thrown at the bailiff.

A vehicle had to be repossessed because the owner had failed to keep up weekly payments. The bailiff and a colleague initially visited with police officers. After it was explained that the vehicle had to be repossessed, the owner appeared to accept this and the police withdrew. The man then became violent and kicked and punched the bailiff and her removal colleague, before starting a petrol-driven cutter, threatening to cut anyone who tried to remove the vehicle. The bailiffs withdrew and called the police who returned to arrest the man. He later pleaded guilty to assault.

SECURITY AND ENFORCEMENT

Bailiffs   Case study 6

REDUCING THE RISK

Training and information

- Staff are encouraged to remain impartial and objective.

- Staff try to avoid confrontation, to be courteous and treat people with understanding and sympathy.

- If someone becomes aggressive, staff are trained to stand sideways to the person to present as small a target as possible and to appear non-threatening.

Work environment

- Protective clothing is worn to protect against dog bites and syringe injuries. Staff do not wear ties or scarves which can be grabbed.

- Staff ensure there is a safe means of escape (eg parking their car facing outwards from a cul-de-sac, or by leaving gates ajar).

Job design

- Staff plan for each assignment by:
  - reading the documents to ensure that they are correct and properly empower the bailiff;
  - considering whether any assistance from colleagues will be needed;
  - ensuring the respondent fully understands what is happening and what may occur in the future.

- If attacked, the bailiff backs away immediately and leaves the address.

- Mobile phones are used with precise map location to summon assistance.

- Joint visits with the police are arranged if trouble is anticipated.

- Staff carry as little cash as possible.

- Staff ensure that their office/back-up knows precisely where they are.

OTHER OPTIONS

- Ensure up to date anti-tetanus injections to protect in case of dog bites.

- Wear clothing without external pockets.

- Make use of body belts to carry personal items.

- For work-related papers, use bags which can be worn across the body rather than on the shoulder.

- Make use of mobile phones, with pre-set numbers for use in emergencies.

REDUCING THE RISK

SECURITY AND ENFORCEMENT

Case study 7   Security officers

BACKGROUND

Research has shown that security staff have a particularly high risk of being assaulted or becoming victims of abuse and threats. Work often involves protecting isolated sites, 24 hours a day.

The security service in this case study employs around 200 security officers on 50 sites, guarding factories, offices and warehouses. It has had only two staff assaults in the 14 years since it was founded.

The female founder and Chief Executive sets the operating culture in the organisation. Her mission is to deliver a quality service and protect her staff – even when the focus on staff protection means losing contracts.

KEY RISKS

KEY RISKS

- Assault, injury (including from needles), threats and abuse.

- Theft and damage of personal property.

Example of incident

A number of security officers were working at a large industrial site. People arrived outside the site to meet workers and a car stopped beside the manual barrier. A passenger left the vehicle and, without warning, hit the guard on duty, then lifted the barrier and allowed the car to enter. A female security officer responded to a call for assistance. She spoke to the car driver. Suddenly the passenger headbutted the officer, lifted the barrier and jumped back in the car after it passed through. The car then drove away at speed.

SECURITY AND ENFORCEMENT

Security officers   Case study 7

REDUCING THE RISK

Training and information

- Unsuitable staff are filtered out through selection, training and induction procedures.

- The organisation provides the Security Industry Training Organisation (SITO) training package for recruits, followed by 13 weeks supervised and structured on-the-job training.

- Performance assessment includes adherence to personal safety routines.

- During formal and on-the-job training, recruits are taught to be non-confrontational in approach. Various styles and techniques involving courtesy, politeness, being firm but fair, smiling and helpful are drilled into staff.

- Continual on-the-job monitoring of individual performance is carried out.

Work environment

- The company make use of equipment and procedures to enhance the safety of their staff, such as a 24-hour control room with audio/visual monitoring of sites and staff.

- The client must provide adequate safety arrangements for guards. These could include suitable perimeter fences, offices or gatehouses, CCTV coverage of remote areas, additional staff, provision of radios and mobile phones for communication, and guard dogs. Unless sufficient safety arrangements are agreed, the work is declined.

- Staff have current anti-tetanus injections.

Job design

- Staff operate in pairs or teams with random supervisory checks.

- Mobile patrols are used as back-up.

- Staff stay in regular contact with the control room.

OTHER OPTIONS

- Provision of personal alarms and/or electronic personnel tracking devices.

- Availability of counselling and self-defence sessions for staff.

REDUCING THE RISK

SECURITY AND ENFORCEMENT

25

SECTOR: LEISURE/SERVICE PROVIDERS

There are a wide range of occupations within this sector, and all involve a high level of face-to-face contact with members of the public. The British Crime Survey identifies several situations in which violence tends to arise:

- The provider of the service decides to withdraw the service from an individual - for example, asking a customer to leave the premises.

- The recipient of the service is unhappy with the quality of the service.

- Customers may fraudulently try to obtain goods or services with stolen credit cards or cheques.

- High levels of alcohol consumption or drug abuse.

Leisure/service providers case studies

8 Market research

9 Nightclub

10 Sports ground

LEISURE/SERVICE PROVIDERS

Case study 8   Market research

BACKGROUND

Market research includes gathering social data in person or by telephone, product sampling in people's homes or in the streets, and covertly assessing quality of service in shops.

The organisation in this case study is based in a large city. It has forty women interviewers working part-time, covering a large geographical area. Many of the interviewers work alone.

The duties of the team include carrying out interviews on doorsteps, within homes and in public places. The risk of violence is increased if clients select particularly difficult geographic and social areas, or suggest questions which have the potential to annoy or antagonise people.

KEY RISKS

- Threats - from groups of people who congregate during street interviews.

- Verbal abuse - when those interviewed become upset by the questions asked.

- Physical violence - from people trying to take free samples.

- Theft from the person - stealing free samples being carried during surveys.

- Theft of or from cars - from people hoping to find free samples.

- Damage to cars - stones may be thrown at cars as they drive away.

Examples of incidents

One woman reported being attacked by youths and her handbag containing samples stolen.

Women researchers said they occasionally received propositions from people they interviewed, or they sometimes felt uneasy as the interview progressed.

During an ice cream tasting, although there was more than enough to go round, some people became impatient and others wanted more than one sample. The jostling crowd put younger children at risk so the event had to be closed quickly.

LEISURE/SERVICE PROVIDERS

Market research   Case study 8

REDUCING THE RISK

Training and information

- The recruitment manager explains to interviewees the problems they may experience. She tries to expose trainees to as wide and representative a sample of tasks and settings to provide a realistic induction into the work.

- Staff are trained to look out for cues to potential problems. They also share information about difficult areas and situations.

- Staff are trained to smile and be friendly. If in doubt about a person's mood, the staff are told to apologise for disturbing them and leave.

- Staff are told to be truthful at all times and to explain to respondents that any information given would be treated confidentially.

- Staff are told not to challenge any answers, other than seeking clarification, as this may annoy respondents.

- Researchers are told they have the right to terminate an interview if they feel unsafe.

Work environment

- Researchers prefer viewing tests or 'hall' tests which involve an invited audience in a single location together with a team of researchers.

- When entering a home, interviewers try to seat themselves or stand where they have a clear view of the room, its exit and the interviewee.

- Mobile phones are carried, but they are often turned off when the interview begins.

- Dressing down rather than up means that interviewers are able to merge with people within a specific area.

Job design

- Researchers are told to call on their manager to assist if there are specific problems.

- Researchers try to park their cars where they can see them.

OTHER OPTIONS

- It may be safer to carry samples in carrier bags instead of handbags, as they would not be so easily recognisable.

- Researchers should be encouraged not to turn off mobile phones during interviews. A pre-set device can be used to call the office in case of emergency.

- Researchers should make sure they let their manager know where they are at all times, particularly if working in a known problem area.

REDUCING THE RISK

LEISURE/SERVICE PROVIDERS

Case study 9   Nightclub

BACKGROUND

Acity nightclub has been operating for 10 years and is licensed to hold just under 1000 people. It opens from 10 pm to 2 am on Thursday, Friday and Saturday nights.

It employs 50 staff, of which 16 act as stewards, with 10 patrolling inside the club and at least 7 bar staff.

A nurse is always on duty and 20 staff have been trained in first aid. Staff turnover is low.

The club has a strong policy on dealing with drugs on the premises and now has a reputation as a 'drugs-free' zone.

KEY RISKS

- Threats and abuse – from customers waiting to get into the club.

- Assaults – staff may have to intervene in fights, or remove troublemakers.

- Robbery – staff have to handle large amounts of cash.

- Sexual harassment.

Example of incident

Staff are sometimes assaulted when they intervene to prevent fighting between clubbers, or when they remove offensive weapons from people, or if they have to escort troublemakers from the premises.

KEY RISKS

LEISURE/SERVICE PROVIDERS

Nightclub   Case study 9

REDUCING THE RISK

Training and information

- Staff are trained to enforce strict control of customers entering the club:
  - admission is limited to those who are sober and not under the influence of drugs;
  - people are searched on admission, including the use of a metal detector;
  - licensed opening times are strictly enforced.

- Staff are trained to be non-provocative, and to let the stewards handle difficult customers.

- Stewards are trained in customer service and how to remove or restrain with minimal force.

- There are nightly briefings for stewards to exchange information on troublemakers and those banned from the premises.

- The club publicises its rules about immediate removal for fighting, causing annoyance, being drunk or found in possession of drugs. All of these could lead to customers being barred in future.

Work environment

- There is a raised cash desk to keep money out of sight.

- Low lighting is used to provide intimacy but allow sufficient visibility.

- Emergency back-up lighting and tamper-proof switches have been installed.

- Some areas of the club are kept closed until the number of customers requires more supervised space.

- Visible CCTV cameras have been installed to provide high quality recordings to aid police investigations or prosecutions.

Job design

- Sufficient staff are always available to serve and control the customers – eg several bar staff are working at any one time to reduce waiting times for drinks.

- Empty glasses are collected promptly so they cannot be used as weapons.

- Stewards are deployed in high profile at key points, and keep in contact visually and by radio. Stewards wear a distinctive uniform with their role written on the jacket.

OTHER OPTIONS

- Staff encouraged to be friendly and welcoming to customers and to adopt a non-confrontational approach to troublemakers.

- Staff trained to stand sideways to difficult customers to present as small a target as possible.

- Staff share information on potential troublemakers.

- Premises kept clean to give impression of good management.

- When intervening, staff stay within sight of other staff members.

REDUCING THE RISK

LEISURE/SERVICE PROVIDERS

Case study 10 Sports ground

BACKGROUND

This case study features a small professional football club. It has a capacity of 16 000, but on most match days the numbers attending are much smaller. The club has three all-seater stands and one standing area.

The club has over 100 stewards who are provided with a uniform. Their role is to offer help to spectators and to assist the police in crowd control. There is a part-time safety officer who is responsible for all aspects of crowd safety, compliance with fire and other regulations, police liaison and managing the stewards.

The risks managed by the club are similar to those for other larger professional football clubs, but usually less frequent and serious. Local police often allow matches to be played without their attendance. The policing role is then carried out by club stewards.

KEY RISKS

- Crowd disorder – in the stands and outside the ground, particularly between rival supporters.

- Pitch invasions.

- Assaults on staff, including injuries from missiles.

- Physical threats and abuse to staff – particularly when the home team loses.

- Verbal threats and abuse.

- Robbery – when handling large amounts of cash on match days.

Examples of incidents

On one occasion staff were trapped in a building and were threatened by an angry crowd following a home defeat.

A known troublemaker was deliberately standing on a seat during a match. A steward approached him, smiled and gestured to him to sit down. The troublemaker did so immediately, without a reaction.

KEY RISKS

LEISURE/SERVICE PROVIDERS

Sports ground   Case study 10

REDUCING THE RISK

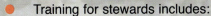

Training and information

- The selection process for stewards stresses that the role has a risk of threats and assaults.

- Training for stewards includes:
  - communication skills and customer care;
  - stop and search techniques;
  - surveillance of crowds;
  - use of reasonable force.

- The club safety officer briefs stewards before every match, reminding them of their training in customer care and providing information from police on potential troublemakers.

- Stewards are debriefed after each match to identify any potential crowd control improvements for future matches.

- Club policy on violence includes:
  - random searches for alcohol or weapons as spectators enter the ground;
  - those who are drunk or who refuse to be searched are refused entry;
  - alcohol is banned in the ground;
  - disorderly spectators are removed and prevented from re-entering for the remainder of the match;
  - those convicted of violence are banned from the ground.

Work environment

- Rival supporters are segregated in the stands.

- A temporary extending tunnel is used to protect players and officials as they enter or leave the pitch.

- CCTV is used inside the stadium.

Job design

- Stewards use radios to exchange information and manage deployments during the match.

- Stewards are each issued with a call sign during pre-match briefings.

- Stewards are updated by radio on the mood of supporters and given information from the police mingling with the fans.

OTHER OPTIONS

- Credit card ticket purchases to reduce risk of cash robbery.

- All cash securely collected and transported to the bank.

REDUCING THE RISK

LEISURE/SERVICE PROVIDERS

Work-related violence case studies: Managing the risk in smaller businesses

FURTHER INFORMATION

GENERAL GUIDANCE

Violence at work: A guide for employers Leaflet INDG69(rev)
HSE Books 1996 (single copy free or priced packs of 10 ISBN 0 7176 1271 6)

Barry Poyner and Caroline Warne *Preventing violence to staff*
HSE Books 1988 ISBN 0 11 885467 4

SECTOR GUIDANCE

Preventing violence to retail staff HSG133
HSE Books 1995 ISBN 0 7176 0891 3

Prevention of violence to staff in banks and building societies
HSG100 HSE Books 1993 ISBN 0 7176 0683 X

Violence in the education sector Education Service Advisory Committee,
HSE Books 1997 ISBN 0 7176 1293 7

Violence and aggression to staff in health services: Guidance on assessment and management Health Services Advisory Committee
HSE Books 1997 ISBN 0 7176 1466 2

FOUR-STAGE MANAGEMENT APPROACH

Health risk management: A practical guide for managers in small and medium-sized enterprises HSG137 HSE Books 1995 ISBN 0 7176 0905 7

RESEARCH

H Standing and D Nicolini *Review of workplace-related violence* CRR143
HSE Books 1997 ISBN 0 7176 1401 8

T Budd *Violence at work: Findings from the British Crime Survey* Home Office
1999 ISBN 1 84082 348 8

T Budd *Violence at work: New findings from the 2000 British Crime Survey*
Home Office 2001. Available only on Home Office website:
http://www.homeoffice.gov.uk/rds/pdfs/occ-violence.pdf

Work-related violence in small and medium-sized businesses Poyner
Research 2000. Available to view at HSE Information Centres.

OTHER INFORMATION

Victims of crime Home Office 2002. Available from police stations, Citizens
Advice Bureaux and victim support schemes.

FURTHER INFORMATION

35

Printed and published by the Health and Safety Executive 6/02 C60